Russia & China in Prophecy

Statesmen could know. Those involved in international affairs could be forewarned. Here, according to Bible prophecy, is what lies ahead for the U.S.S.R. and the nations and peoples on the outer rim of Asia.

D0027583

This booklet is not to be sold. It is a free educational service in the public interest, published by the Worldwide Church of God.

Cover: Norman Merritt-PT
Page 1: Original text by Gene Hogberg
© 1987 Worldwide Church of God
Page 6: Original text by Keith W. Stump
© 1985 Worldwide Church of God
Page 15: Original text by Herbert W. Armstrong (1892-1986)
© 1948 Worldwide Church of God
Page 30: Original text by Keith W. Stump
© 1980 Worldwide Church of God
All Rights Reserved
Printed in U.S.A.

ISBN 0-943093-21-X

RADICALLY ALTERING EUROPE

T wo new words have entered the English language as a result of a dramatic cultural and economic transformation now underway inside the Soviet Union.

The first one, the most familiar, is *glasnost,* roughly translated as "openness." It reflects the new, more open spirit of candor on the part of Soviet officials both in dealing with the West and in permitting greater latitudes of public expression inside the traditionally rigid Soviet society.

The other word is *perestroika,* which means "reconstruction." It has to do with initiatives instituted by Communist Party General Secretary Mikhail Gorbachev and like-minded associates in the Soviet hierarchy to reform the encrusted Soviet economy. They are determined to place it on a firmer, more cost-effective foundation to meet the challenges of the decades ahead.

Openness in the Media, Arts

Glasnost has been reflected in a number of ways, among them:

• Greater latitudes in the official news media, so much so that the distribution of *Pravda,* the Soviet Communist Party newspaper, is not permitted in various parts of more restrictive Eastern Europe. On an official visit to Moscow, British Prime Minister Margaret Thatcher was permitted to speak her frank mind on a late-night telecast.

• For the first time in the U.S.S.R., a display of open political dissent. A group of Crimean Tatars were allowed to demonstrate in Red Square, and were even granted their demand to talk to Soviet President Andrei Gromyko. Small numbers of Tatars, banished to Siberia for alleged pro-Nazi sentiments during World War II, may be permitted to return. In addition, for the first time, ethnic Russians, not just Soviet minorities, may be permitted to emigrate.

• The appearance in concert of an American "pop-rock" artist performing music that was until recently frowned upon by Soviet authorities (who have however looked the other way at the mushrooming of locally established musical groups).

• The distribution of once-banned books such as Boris Pasternak's *Dr. Zhivago* and Anatoli Rybakov's *Children of Arbat,* the latter a fictionalized and sympathetic account of an exiled dissident student under the harsh reign of Stalin.

• The popularity of the movie "Repentance," also a thinly disguised attack on Stalinism.

Of course many restrictions on the lives of Soviet citizens remain, such as the generalized ban on travel to the West. And certainly there is no attempt under the panoply of *glasnost* to diminish the unchallenged role of the Communist Party.

> **The multi-faceted Gorbachev renovation program is making a sizeable impression on the nations of Western Europe.**

Economic Reform

Even more important than *glasnost,* many observers believe, is Mr. Gorbachev's attempt at *perestroika,* the radical reformation of the moribund Soviet economy.

A watershed decision was made by the Communist Party Central Committee in June 1987. After hearing a blistering attack on the country's economic ills from Mr. Gorbachev, the Committee endorsed the General Secretary's overall plan to introduce decentralization of the economy. Its purpose? To allow decision-making so that the Soviet economy becomes more responsive to the realities of the marketplace. The shift away from centralized planning is scheduled to be fully implemented by the end of 1990.

Experts realize a gigantic amount of inertia must be overcome to put the new policy into effect. Yet, Mr. Gorbachev is determined to see his ideas through.

Some skeptics believe that Mr. Gorbachev could face the same fate of an earlier reforming General Secretary, Nikita Khrushchev, who was ousted in 1964. But most Kremlin-watchers stress that times are different today, that even many Soviet political conservatives realize that something drastic has to be done to revive the Soviet economy.

Cultivate European Ties

The multi-faceted Gorbachev renovation program is making a sizeable impression on the nations of Western Europe.

One of the General Secretary's chief lieutenants in the reform program is Aleksandr Yakovlev, the Politburo member in charge of culture and propaganda. One Western analyst goes so far as to say the Gorbachev program is "pure Yakovlev."

Mr. Yakovlev is said by one Western diplomat to have "the profoundest misgivings about everything American." He once described the U.S. as a land of "deep amorality built on a convulsive worship of success."

Mr. Yakovlev, on the other hand, shows great interest in developing relations with Western Europe and Japan. His strategy aims at tapping these areas in order to close the U.S.S.R.'s industrial and technological gap.

The Western Europe connection is certain to develop into a formidable relationship. It is in this area that Mikhail Gorbachev has emerged as a first-rate politician, often stunning his counterparts in Washington and other Western capitals with his astuteness.

Mr. Gorbachev's approach has generally been to take the West up on a series of old proposals made when NATO was convinced previous Soviet leaders would reject them. A top French official told the *Wall Street Journal* (June 17, 1987): "We booby-trapped ourselves. Gorbachev pulled the right string, and the whole thing unraveled. Beautiful. Well played."

Now some observers are wondering whether the shrewd Soviet leader just might take Mr. Reagan up on the latter's plea in front of the Brandenburg Gate and Berlin Wall in mid-1987. "Mr. Gorbachev, open this gate! Mr. Gorbachev, tear down this wall!"

Even a partial opening of the Berlin Wall, constructed over a quarter-century ago, would send shockwaves through Western capitals.

According to one West German policy maker, Gorbachev has "already got all of us Germans talking about reunification, without actually having done or said anything."

Initiatives in East Bloc

It is not only the West that is in for a few surprises. The twin policies of *glasnost* and *perestroika* have proven to be extremely unsettling to the current leaderships of the Soviet-bloc nations of Eastern and Central Europe.

In an unusual twist of fate, the leadership circles of nearly all the other Communist nations in Europe are now out of step with the reform-minded men in Moscow. While they pay lip service to the Kremlin's calls for the entire bloc to institute pragmatic reforms, nearly all of them are dragging their feet.

In the supreme irony of all, the Soviets are pressing Czechoslovakia to effect reforms very similar to what the Czechs were introducing in the late 1960s—before Soviet and Warsaw Pact tanks rolled in to put an end to what was known then as the "Prague Spring." Asked to explain the difference between Gorbachev's "Moscow Spring" and the "Prague Spring" of 1968, Soviet spokesman Gennadi Gerasimov has replied in two memorable words: "Nineteen years."

But for the East bloc leaders, much more is at stake in their own countries, most of which are much more Western in culture and are Communist only as a result of the post-World War II division of Europe. Reforms in Eastern Europe could more easily get out of hand than in the U.S.S.R.

Radically Altered Europe

For several reasons, the status quo of the post-World War II period in Europe, in place for over four decades, is coming to an end. A new set of dynamic conditions, many of them generated in Moscow, is taking over.

In addition, the United States, increasingly preoccupied with Asia, Latin America and the Middle East, is undergoing a fundamental change in its economic and security relationship with Europe.

The removal of U.S. medium-range missiles from Europe, it is widely believed, could generate a momentum leading to a gradual removal of U.S. ground forces.

Western European nations such as France and West Germany are discussing numerous plans to develop a closer defense strategy. They know, said one analyst, "that the long week-end under America's atomic umbrella is drawing to a close."

Out of it all, a much greater relationship between a more unified Western Europe and the Soviet sphere appears inevitable. West German officials continually emphasize that the key to German unification lies in overcoming the political division of Europe as a whole. Under terms of a generalized European settlement, Moscow might consent to much greater political latitude for parts of Eastern Europe.

The big question is what the United States—on the outside looking in—will do when confronted with a new reality straddling the old East-West divide in Europe.

WHAT'S PROPHESIED FOR RUSSIA AND CHINA

The decades-long split between Asia's two communist giants is one of the most crucial variables in world power politics today. What does it mean?

Strategic planners well understand that a settlement of their dispute would radically transform the entire global balance of power. Even a localized *war*—presently unthinkable—between the Soviet Union and China would have equally grave international repercussions.

What's behind the Sino-Soviet quarrels? What lies ahead for the Soviet Union and China—yes, and even India, Japan and Southeast Asia?

Newsmen and diplomats do not know.

War of Words

It was February 1950, in the midst of a freezing Russian winter. Mao Tse-tung (Mao Zedong) stood beaming in a Moscow railway station at the conclusion of a two-month stay in the Soviet Union.

Bundled in a heavy fur coat and wearing a woolen cap, the Chairman of the Chinese People's Republic paused briefly before boarding his train to speak to the onlooking crowd.

Having just concluded a mutual defense treaty with the Kremlin and having received his new nation's first foreign loan for $300 million, he confidently declared that Chinese-

Soviet friendship would be "everlasting, indestructible and inalienable."

It turned out to be one of history's unfulfilled predictions.

By 1963, the friendship lay in ruins. Since then, Sino-Soviet relations have been on ice.

Over the past two decades, the Kremlin has openly criticized aspects of Chinese policy as being "divisive" and at variance with socialist principles and standards. For their part, the Chinese have been equally critical of the Soviet model of socialism, labeling Moscow "a renegade capitalist regime."

At its simplest, the central issue of the Sino-Soviet quarrel is *who is going to be in charge* in the communist world.

The Soviet Union—the world's largest country in land area—claims ultimate supremacy with the whole communist world. China—the world's most populous country—challenges this alleged Soviet hegemony over the world communist movement by offering an alternative mother party.

This ideological struggle continues throughout the world to this day. On both sides, the former days of communist solidarity are now but a dim memory.

Deep Roots

Let's first look at the quarrel through Soviet eyes.

Russia's "Chinaphobia" is by no means a recent phenomenon, nor solely a concoction of modern Kremlin thinkers. The roots of modern-day Sino-Soviet hostility extend deep into the past.

Russians have never forgotten Genghis Khan's Golden Horde, and the Tatar-Mongol occupation of Russia that lasted for some 300 years. Those black years of Mongol domination are deeply rooted in Russia's historical memory. (The Mongols, of course, were not Chinese, but Russians make little distinction between the varied peoples of the East.)

Diplomats in Moscow observe that the Russians are *obsessed* with a fear of the East.

China's staggering population of *one thousand million*

people is more than *three times* that of the Soviet Union! One Soviet academician once observed that, from Russia's viewpoint, their situation vis-a-vis China would be analogous to the United States having a thousand million Mexican neighbors—with nuclear weapons capacity!

This demographic fear of China is indelibly ingrained in the Russian national consciousness. It is instinctive and possibly exaggerated—but to Russians, it is very *real.*

The Chinese suffer from the counterpart of Russia's Sinophobia—namely, Russophobia.

Invoking images of centuries past, Peking writers graphically picture the Russians as a restless people, brooding just outside the Great Wall.

For years, the Chinese feared that their country might be subjected to a Czechoslovak-type invasion by the U.S.S.R. China consequently developed a civil defense system of immense scope. The Chinese citizenry was encouraged to "dig tunnels deep, store grain everywhere and prepare for war."

The heated battle of words continues, with varying intensity, across the long Sino-Soviet border. Historic enmities are not easily shaken off.

Border Controversy

Today's Sino-Soviet tensions are partly an outgrowth of a long-standing Chinese claim to vast stretches of territory now in Soviet hands in the Far East and Central Asia.

These territories were ceded to Czar Alexander II of Russia by China's weak Manchu emperors more than a century ago. Peking maintains that the 19th-century territorial agreements were "unequal treaties" imposed on China by a stronger Czarist Russia.

The Kremlin strongly rejects this claim, declaring that "the territories which Peking qualifies as so-called Chinese lands" were "actually never part of the Chinese state nor was their population Chinese." The history of the demarcation of the Sino-Soviet border, Moscow asserts, was "a long and complex one," and "the fact remains that Russia never seized any Chinese territory."

Even the extent of China's territorial claim is not entirely clear. Over the years, figures for the size of the disputed—

area have ranged from 33,000 square kilometers (13,000 square miles) to 1.5 million square kilometers (577,000 square miles)—a vast area more than twice the size of Texas.

Included in the disputed area are the strategic city of Vladivostok and much of the immense Soviet republic of Kazakhstan.

Concern over the Sino-Soviet border dispute reached its high point in March 1969. In that month, the controversy erupted into armed fighting on a disputed island in the ice-bound Ussuri River north of Vladivostok.

The clash in the bleak snow-swept wilderness of eastern Asia involved at least a battalion of men on each side. It resulted in the deaths of more than 30 Soviet border guards and an unknown number of Chinese. The two nations appeared to be on a collision course, hovering close to full-scale war!

In November 1972, came another border clash, this time thousands of miles to the west. It took the lives of at least five Soviet soldiers and several shepherds near the historic Dzungarian Gate. This "gate," used by Genghis Khan when he led his army into the West, is a natural mountain pass joining Soviet Kazakhstan and China's strategic Sinkiang (Xinjiang) province.

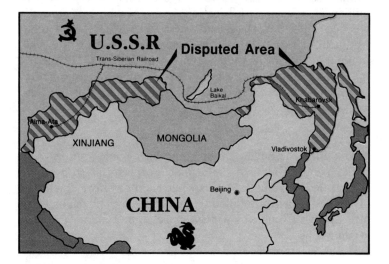

In subsequent years, literally *dozens* of armed skirmishes have taken place in these remote disputed areas. The last round of border talks was broken off seven years ago.

Some experts believe that the two nations have entered a classic prewar situation.

Major Arms Buildup

The Sino-Soviet borderlands are heavily fortified on both sides.

It is estimated that the Soviet Union has nearly *a third* of its entire 4.5-million-man army positioned on or near the Russian-Chinese frontier. These Soviet troops are armed with the latest weapons and nuclear missiles. Also, the Soviet Union now has nearly 2,000 advanced aircraft in defensive position should a crisis occur with either China or Japan.

China's military preparations are numerically impressive. China has the world's second largest armed force—the 4.1-million-man People's Liberation Army. Much of its strength is concentrated near the sensitive border with the Soviet Union. And China now has missiles capable of hitting Moscow, Leningrad and other major centers in European Russia.

Some military analysts believe that the preparations on the Sino-Soviet border represent the biggest arms buildup the world has ever seen!

Soviet Nuclear Blitz?

At one time the Soviet Union could have made a preemptive strike against China with reasonable expectation of destroying her fledgling nuclear bases while running only a small risk of Chinese nuclear retaliation. A preemptive Soviet nuclear blitz against China was widely expected by military analysts at that time.

But Western defense officials say today that the Soviet

Union, under warning from the United States, missed its chance to destroy China's nuclear program while it was still safe to do so. China, as one observer put it, has long since "grown out of its atomic diapers."

In view of Russia's diminishing nuclear advantage, diplomatic sources in Europe and Asia today virtually dismiss the possibility of a Russian preemptive strike against China. The Kremlin, they say, would not risk such a dangerous policy in the face of the present odds.

True, the U.S.S.R. still has both qualitative and quantitative nuclear superiority. But China, apart from her nuclear factor, also has *manpower!*

Kremlin planners realize that a vigorous Chinese counterattack would be *certain*—a nuclear counterattack if still possible, but unquestionably a massive *land* attack!

The chances are high that the Soviets would quickly find themselves embroiled in a protracted "Vietnam-type" situation in China—a long conventional land war fueled by the tenaciousness and determination of the Chinese people to defend the motherland.

The Chinese have publicly vowed to fight a 100-year war, if necessary, to achieve victory in any Sino-Soviet conflict that might erupt. The enemy, Peking has declared, would ultimately be "drowned in the ocean of a people's war."

The specter of multiple millions of Chinese flooding across the border in a mammoth guerrilla campaign fills Kremlin strategists' nights with dread. Such a scenario is too horrible for the average Russian to contemplate.

As one Western military expert observed a few years ago: "If Russia went into China, she may never come out."

In his "Letter to the Soviet Leaders," Alexander Solzhenitsyn said that a war with China would last 10 to 15 years and would cost Russia at least *60 million* dead. The risks of a Soviet strike against China are clearly prohibitive. Such a war would be futile and counterproductive for all concerned.

An unwanted accidental conflict—sparked by unforeseen causes and escalating quickly out of control—always remains a possibility. Such a conflict could conceivably remain non-nuclear and be limited to action in border regions. But even limited fighting of this sort is generally considered unlikely.

Sino-Soviet Détente?

If war has indeed become unthinkable between the two communist superpowers, what are the prospects for *reconciliation?*

Can the Sino-Soviet split be patched up?

Decades of quarreling over frontiers and other issues will not quickly be put aside, but the Sino-Soviet dispute is not necessarily fixed in concrete. Indeed, both sides are well aware of the enormous advantages that could be realized by reconciliation.

For both the Chinese and the Soviets, détente would allow a reduction of their crushingly burdensome military expenditures. It would also greatly bolster their leverage in the international political arena.

Will it happen? And in what circumstances?

A renewal of negotiations could yet eliminate the nettlesome boundary issue. The ideological issue—that of who will dominate world communism—would prove a thornier problem, though some sort of compromise or accommodation might be hammered out if sufficient motivation were present on both sides.

It should be remembered that neither side has sought to sever diplomatic relations during their decades-long feud. Even Sino-Soviet trade has continued.

Many Kremlinologists and China-watchers, however, feel that both sides are *privately* interested in a cautious normalization of relations over the long term.

Eurasian Colossus?

What does Bible prophecy reveal for the future of Asian relations? In numerous prophecies, the Bible points to the development of a *giant Eurasian* world power, linked with populous neighbors by military and/or political alliances.

Almost 2,000 years ago, the aged apostle John saw in vision armies totaling *200 million men*—armies that will sweep across Europe and critical battlefronts elsewhere, devastating the final restoration of the old Roman Empire that will have emerged just before the end of this age (Rev. 9:16).

These great armies—which could be mustered only by combining the forces of the Soviet Union and the Asian allies—are alluded to by the prophet Daniel (Dan. 11:44). He recorded that a sphere of power to the east and north of the Holy Land (where Soviet Russia is today) would become involved in a struggle, with the revived Roman Empire in Europe, for control of the Eastern Mediterranean.

Consider, now, *how* political alliances in Eurasia might come into being.

The Soviet Union has a long-standing fear of one day being caught up in a *two-front* war—a simultaneous conflict with both Europe and China. Kremlin planners will do virtually anything to prevent that.

> **The central issue of the Sino-Soviet quarrel is who is going to be in charge in the communist world.**

Worsening relations with China on her eastern flank, coupled with Eastern Europe's severe drain on Soviet economic and military resources, could eventually make it necessary for the Soviet Union to *loosen its hold* on Eastern Europe.

The Kremlin may have to strike a political deal that would bring about the withdrawal of its military forces from Eastern Europe, for duty in Asia, and allow countries from Eastern Europe to associate themselves with the evolving West European union. This would create the circumstances necessary for the final emergence of a United Europe—the final restoration of the Roman Empire—as a major world power.

Already, Moscow's buildup of military forces along the Chinese border has weakened her strategic position in Europe and undermined her control over Eastern Europe.

But any such Russo-European "accommodation" would not last.

Ultimately, as the prophesied United Europe rises to global super-powerdom, a fearful Kremlin would be forced to settle its differences with China—to be free to deal with rising *European* religious, political and military leadership.

However it happens, Russia and Asian neighbors *will* ultimately find themselves in some degree joining forces out of necessity to confront a power they perceive as challenging the triumph of world communism.

Future developments in Soviet-Chinese and Sino-Indian relations will have profound and far-reaching repercussions for the entire world. Their relationships will play a large part in molding the shape of world events as the final years of this age draw near.

WHY RUSSIA WILL NOT ATTACK AMERICA

F or decades now, the prospect of war between Russia and the United States has continually heightened and lessened.

Some who claim to be authorities on prophecy assure people a war involving Russia and the United States, Canada and Britain is prophesied in Ezekiel 38.

The United States and Canada and the democracies of northwestern Europe they recognize as the nations descended from the so-called lost Ten Tribes of Israel. Therefore, they conclude, the prophecy of Ezekiel 38 of Gog attacking the land of Israel foretells a military invasion of the North American continent from the Soviet Union.

Others claim it foretells an *imminent* Soviet invasion of the Middle East. But this is *not* what the prophecy says.

What Ezekiel 38 does foretell is truly astounding.

Time Sequence of Ezekiel's Prophecy

Ezekiel's message is for our day—a prophetic warning for America and Britain, now!

To understand the time, the place and all the facts of the prophecy of Ezekiel 38, we need to begin at the first chapter of Ezekiel's prophecy and read the book clear through.

When we do this, we find a time sequence flowing through the book.

Notice, in the very first verse, Ezekiel was among the Jewish captives who had been taken from Judah to the river Chebar. It was in the fifth year of the captivity of King Jehoiachin that this prophecy began coming to Ezekiel through visions.

Ezekiel was being shown things far into the future.

Notice, the prophecy was inspired and written *after* Judah's captivity began—about 130 years after the House of Israel had been taken captive to Assyria.

Yet, Ezekiel is a prophet to the House of Israel. (Not to be confused with the modern Jewish nation of Israel. These Israelis are actually descendants of ancient Judah.) His prophecy applies to the far future—*not* to the captivity of ancient Israel, which had occurred more than 130 years before he wrote.

Notice Ezekiel's message, a prophecy for the future, is primarily for the House of Israel (Ezek. 2:3; 3:1, 4-7).

In chapter 3, verse 17, Ezekiel is made a watchman to warn the House of Israel.

Message to Israel, Not Judah

Notice! Beginning chapter 3: After the prophet "eats the roll"—that is, receives the prophetic warning message—he is to "go speak unto the house of Israel"—not to the Jews among whom he dwelt.

Remember he is already among the captives of Judah. But he is told: "Go, get thee unto the house of Israel" (verse 4).

The 12 tribes of Israel had long before this divided into *two nations*—the 10 tribes being the House of Israel, while Judah, Benjamin and Levi composed the House of Judah, who, only, were "Jews."

The Jewish people of today are descended from the House of Judah. But the English-speaking racial descendants of Joseph composing the United States, Canada, Britain, Australia and New Zealand are the leading "birthright" tribes of Ephraim and Manasseh, heads of the 10 tribes of the House of Israel. Ezekiel's message is for *our* day—and it is, therefore, a message for these peoples, NOW!

Notice chapter 4. The prophet is to place before him a

tile, and trace upon it the city of Jerusalem, and "lay siege" against it. The war pictured was against Jerusalem, capital of Judah. But "this" (verse 3) "shall be a sign to the house of Israel." Then follows the well-known key to the "day for a year" method of reckoning prophecy.

Continue chapter 5: "... For," comes the warning message from the Eternal, "thereof shall a fire come forth into all the house of Israel" (verse 4). Notice, this is to portray vividly a warning of some FUTURE destruction upon the House of Israel! Not upon Judah, already largely conquered by Nebuchadnezzar. But upon Israel—the 10-tribed

> ## The people finally will cry out for a true prophet or minister of the Eternal God—but it will be too late!

nation who had gone into its first and original captivity 130 long years before! The warning is not of a captivity already history. It says "thereof shall a fire *come*" upon Israel! It is a prophecy relating to a *future* destruction and captivity.

No such destruction and captivity has ever *yet* come to the House of Israel since this was written. Therefore it is still in the future—*in our time.*

A Captivity Yet Future

Notice more of this warning:

"A third part of thee [America-Canada-Britain] shall die with the pestilence, and with famine shall they be consumed in the midst of thee: and a third part shall fall by the sword round about thee; and I will scatter a third part into all the winds [in captivity being removed from their own lands and scattered over the world] ..." (verse 12).

Coming to chapter 6, the local scene of the vision shifts to the mountainous land of ancient Israel, in the Middle East— but the message is for America, Canada and Britain, today.

Will we heed it? God help us to wake up!

"... Behold, I, even I," says the Eternal God (verses 3, 5-7), "will bring a sword [invasion] upon you, and I will destroy your high places.... And I will lay the dead carcases of the children of Israel before their idols; and I will scatter your bones round about your altars. In all your dwelling places the cities *shall be laid waste* [nuclear bombing].... and ye shall know that I am the Lord."

Just a small remnant shall escape and be spared (verse 8). They are described in Luke 21:36.

Continue: "Thus saith the Lord God... Alas for all the evil abominations of [not Judah, but] the house of Israel! for they shall [not *did,* in the captivity 130 years before Ezekiel wrote, but *shall*] fall by the sword, by the famine, and by the pestilence" (verse 11).

The Time Is Yet Future

Notice the time. It's important.

"All hands shall be feeble, and all knees shall be weak as water" (chapter 7, verse 17). "Howl ye; for the day of the Lord is at hand. ... Therefore shall all hands be faint, and every man's heart shall melt: and they shall be afraid..." (Isa. 13:6-8). Plainly, the time is the "Day of the Lord"—yet in the immediate future!

Continue in Ezekiel: "They shall cast their silver in the streets, and their gold shall be removed: their silver and their gold shall not be able to deliver them in the day of the wrath of the Lord..." (Ezek. 7:19). Now compare that with Zephaniah 1:14-15, 17-18: "The great day of the Lord is near.... That day is a day of wrath.... And I [the Eternal] will bring distress upon men.... Neither their silver nor their gold shall be able to deliver them in the day of the Lord's wrath...." Both are speaking of the same time—a time shortly ahead of us, in this present generation!

"Wherefore," continues verse 24 (Ezek. 7), "I will bring the worst of the heathen, and they shall possess their houses: I will also make the pomp of the strong to cease.... Destruction cometh; and they shall seek peace, and there shall be none.... Then shall they seek a vision of the prophet; but the law shall perish from the priest" (verses 25-26).

Yes, when this comes, the people finally will cry out for

a true prophet or minister of the Eternal God—but it will be too late! For then shall have come the time spoken of by the prophet Amos, when there shall be a famine of hearing the words of the Eternal—(Amos 8:11)—an end of true gospel preaching. Already the people and their ministers have turned their eyes and ears from God's law.

Notice chapter 11 of Ezekiel's prophecy. It is a message addressed to the House of Israel (verse 5). ". . . I will bring a sword upon you, saith the Lord God. And I will bring you out of the midst thereof, and deliver you into the hands of strangers, and will execute judgments among you. Ye shall fall by the sword . . ." (verses 8-10). When? It is future from the time Ezekiel wrote, and it has not yet happened since then. God says it will happen!

Chapter 12, verse 11: ". . . they shall remove and go into captivity." It is yet future—and it is the House of Israel.

When? "And they shall know that I am the Lord, when I shall scatter them among the nations, and disperse them in the countries" (verse 15). The expression "They shall know that I am the Lord" is used repeatedly through the book of Ezekiel—always referring to the time of the Second Coming of Christ, and Israel's final restoration back to her original land. Many prophecies show that the modern nations descended from ancient Israel are to be scattered in this latter-day captivity when Christ comes to restore them back to that land.

People Won't Believe It

Always the true prophets and ministers of God have stood almost alone and opposed by the overwhelming majority in Israel. That is Israel's history of old. It is true today.

The 13th chapter shows the declaration of the popular ministry of this day in Israel—in the United States, Canada and Britain.

"Son of man, prophesy against the prophets of Israel . . . Woe unto the foolish prophets, that follow their own spirit, and have seen nothing! O Israel, thy prophets are like the foxes in the deserts. Ye have not gone up into the gaps, neither made up the hedge for the house of Israel to stand in the battle in the day of the Lord" (verses 2-5). It is speaking of the soon-coming "Day of the Lord"—not some ancient event! "... they have seduced my people, saying, Peace; and there was no peace ..." (verse 10).

Ezekiel catalogs the nations' sins—customs and ways that seem right but that are contrary to God's laws and an abomination in his sight. Some of them he mentions in the 8th chapter.

And chapter 22: "Thou hast despised mine holy things, and hast profaned my sabbaths," says the Eternal (verse 8). "... thou hast taken usury and increase, and thou hast greedily gained of thy neighbours by extortion, and hast forgotten me, saith the Lord.... And I will [not *did*, but *will*] scatter thee among the heathen, and disperse thee in the countries, and will consume thy filthiness out of thee" (verses 12, 15).

Chapters 25 through 32, Ezekiel digresses to prophesy against a number of foreign nations who have come in direct contact with Israel. In Ezekiel 33:11, the prophet returns to pleading with the House of Israel. "... Turn ye, turn ye," God pleads, "from your evil ways; for why will ye die, O house of Israel?" Here, too, Ezekiel is again directed to be a watchman to warn the House of Israel—THE UNITED STATES, CANADA AND BRITAIN TODAY—at the time when this prophesied foreign sword is coming. Ezekiel wrote the message—but it remains for us to whom God has revealed it today to actually shout and proclaim it

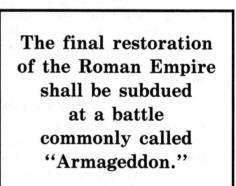

The final restoration of the Roman Empire shall be subdued at a battle commonly called "Armageddon."

to the people. God help us to be faithful in this solemn and grave commission!

In the 34th chapter, God tells him to prophesy against the ministers of our land. They have fed themselves and not the flocks. They have preached what people wanted to hear (II Tim. 4:3-4) in order to get their salaries.

The Coming of Christ!

And now the Eternal inspires the prophet to come to the solution.

"Thus saith the Lord God; Behold, I am against the shepherds; and I will require my flock at their hand, and cause them to cease from feeding the flock. . . . Behold, I, even I, will both search my sheep, and seek them out. . . . And will deliver them out of all places where they have been scattered in the cloudy and dark day [the Day of the Lord— yet future]. And I will . . . gather them from the countries, and will bring them to their own land, and feed them [spiritual food] upon the mountains of Israel by the rivers, and in all the inhabited places of the country" (Ezek. 34:10-13).

Christ himself will set his hand again the second time to recover the remnant of his people Israel (Isa. 11:11). Spiritual blindness shall then be removed, and all Israel shall be saved! (See Romans 11:25-26.) The kingdom of God shall be established. Men shall be tired of their own ways, and seek God's ways—and his law shall go forth of Zion (Mic. 4:2-3). And the nations shall find PEACE!

In the 36th chapter of Ezekiel, the Eternal addresses the House of Israel: "Prophesy unto the mountains of Israel . . . Thus saith the Lord God to the mountains, and to the hills, to the rivers, and to the valleys, to the desolate wastes, and to the cities that are forsaken. . . . But ye, O mountains of Israel, ye shall shoot forth your branches, and yield your fruit to my people of Israel; for they are at hand to come. . . . And I will multiply men upon you, all the house of Israel, even all of it: and the cities shall be inhabited, and the wastes shall be builded: and I will multiply upon you man and beast . . ." (verses 1, 4, 8, 10-11).

Yes, the House of Israel is pictured returning to its original land, *not* from a condition of wealth and prosperity from Britain, the United States and Canada—not in the position of a people victorious in a great world war—but as a slave and captive people, scattered through the nations of the world. All prophecies picturing this rescue and regathering of Israel at Christ's coming give us the same prophetic picture.

Both Houses of Israel United

In chapter 37, the first part pictures the "valley of dry
bones." This represents (verse 11) the whole House of Israel—including Judah. It has a dual significance. It pictures
the rebirth and resurrection of Israel *as a nation,* from
captivity, dispersion and slavery. It pictures, too, the literal
bodily resurrection of the individuals who had already died,
after which the knowledge of the truth—spiritual knowledge—shall be revealed, and they shall be converted, and
God's Spirit shall enter within, and they shall be saved.

Beginning with the 15th verse, the illustration of the two
sticks shows the two houses, or nations, Israel and Judah,
being once more united, under Christ at his Second Coming,
in the land of Israel.

"... Thus saith the Lord God; Behold, I will take the
children of Israel [from the British Isles, America and
Canada—from a position of wealth and affluence as recent
victors in the world war? No, but] from among the heathen,
whither they be gone, and will gather them on every side, and
bring them into their own land: and I will make them one
nation in the land upon the mountains of Israel; and one king
shall be king to them all: and they shall be no more two
nations, neither shall they be divided into two kingdoms any
more at all: neither shall they defile themselves any more
with their idols, nor with their detestable things, nor with any
of their transgressions.... And they shall dwell in the land
that I have given unto Jacob my servant, wherein your
fathers have dwelt... they, and their children, and their
children's children *for ever....* Moreover I will make a
covenant of peace with them; it shall be an *everlasting
covenant* ..."—the New Covenant (verses 21-23, 25-26).

At Peace in the Holy Land

Notice, now the story flow—the time sequence: The prophet
has carried us through the sins of his people, the coming
invasion and captivity and dispersion, and the coming of
Christ as Deliverer to restore the fortunes of Israel. We have
come to the time when both the Houses of Israel and Judah
shall be reunited into one nation, rescued from captivity and

dispersion and regathered in their land, once again made prosperous, having learned their lesson, now living God's way, under his laws, enjoying his richest blessings, both material and spiritual!

And now we come to chapter 38. This chapter finds Israel restored in her land—"the land that is brought back from the sword" (verse 8). We find Israel now at rest, dwelling safely, totally unprepared for war—having "neither bars nor gates" (verse 11), in the desolate places of the land of Israel, now inhabited (verse 12)—yes, inhabited (same verse) by the people who are once again restored to great material prosperity—"which have gotten cattle and goods, that dwell in the midst of the land."

Notice it!

This prophecy does not picture the British Isles, America and Canada. It pictures the Holy Land. It pictures all 12 tribes having been taken there from a dispersion and captivity and slavery, gathered out of the nations where they had been scattered, now once again beginning to prosper.

Notice it: The time of this prophecy is after—not before, but after—the Second Coming of Christ—after the great Deliverer has come and rescued our people and restored us to the land of Israel—after Israel and Judah are reunited. Certainly the "latter years" (verse 8).

The place of this battle is not Britain or America or Canada—it is the Holy Land. ". . . thou shalt come into the land that is brought back from the sword, and is gathered out of many people, against the mountains of Israel, which have been always waste [or "once a perpetual waste"—Moffatt translation]" (verse 8). The "mountains of Israel" is an expression used all through the book of Ezekiel, and refers to the literal mountainous land of ancient Israel.

Our people shall have regained so much wealth that Gog and allies shall come to "take a spoil" (verse 13), "to carry away silver and gold, to take away cattle and goods, to take a great spoil."

Christ's Reign Contested

But this very fact—that this invasion will not come until *after* the Second Coming of Christ—will seem preposterous to many, at first thought. That is because we have been accustomed merely to assume things that are not true. Many have blindly assumed that when Christ comes, there will be no opposition. Every person and power on earth, some have thought, will simply submit meekly and instantly to him and his power. But that is not true!

Some gentile nations understandably shall not submit until forced to. The final restoration of the Roman Empire shall be subdued and conquered at a battle commonly called "Armageddon." But the populous nations of Eurasia that the Almighty God up to this point has not dealt with shall still have to be brought to submission.

"Gog" Identified

"Gog" in the land of "Magog" is the vast regions of the U.S.S.R. in northern Eurasia extending from the Baltic to the Pacific. "Meshech" is Moscow, "Tubal" is Tobol'sk.

Notice the allies who come with them in this future battle. You will find "Gomer," "Togarmah," "Magog," "Meshech," "Tubal" identified in Genesis 10 as the sons of Japheth, father of the Eurasians. Ethiopia and Phut (mistranslated Libya) are descended from Ham.

Therefore, this prophecy of Ezekiel 38 shows who shall finally succeed in marshaling peoples of each major race into a gigantic invasion upon the modern descendants of ancient Israel regathered in their land.

When God begins to rule the world, through Christ— with his chosen people restored to prosperity in the land of Israel, the very center of the land surface of the earth (verse 12, Moffatt translation)—this great Eurasian union of nations shall finally be tempted to use their mighty air force. "Thou shalt ascend," the Eternal says, "and come like a storm [in the air], thou shalt be like a cloud to cover the land . . ." (verse 9). There shall be so many planes then that they will hide the sun from the ground below, like a huge dark shadow!

The End of World Conquest

The House of Israel at that time shall not be armed or prepared. ". . . In that day when my people of Israel dwelleth safely, shalt thou not know it?" asks the Eternal. "And thou shalt come from thy place out of the north parts [due north of the land of ancient Israel], thou, and many people [allies] with thee . . . a mighty army: and thou shalt come up against my people of Israel, as a cloud to cover the land; it shall be in the latter days, and I will bring thee against my land, that the heathen may know me [note the purpose], when I shall be sanctified in thee, O Gog, before their eyes" (verses 14-16).

> Ezekiel's message is for *our* day—and it is, therefore, a message for America, Canada and Britain, NOW!

But the Israelites shall not have to fight in that battle. They shall have learned by then that God fights their battles for them!

"And it shall come to pass at the same time when Gog shall come against the land of Israel, saith the Lord God, that my fury shall come up in my face" (verse 18). "So that . . . all the men that are upon the face of the earth, shall shake at my presence . . ." (verse 20). It is after Christ's coming!

"I will summon an utter panic against him [Gog], says the Lord the Eternal, till every man in his host shall draw the sword against his fellow; I will punish him with pestilence and bloodshed, I will rain on him and his hordes and all the nations in his train an overpowering flood, with hail-stones, fire, and brimstone. I will let all the nations see my might and dread divinity—to teach them that I am the Eternal" (verses 21-23, Moffatt translation).

Notice, these nations do not see and recognize the dread divinity, the might and power of the Eternal Christ, even after he has returned. He has to teach them that HE IS THE ETERNAL!

The 39th chapter shows in more detail the result of this great battle, in which Christ, with supernatural power, causes five sixths of these armies to be slain.

Notice, again, the time: "Now will I bring again the captivity of Jacob, and have mercy upon the whole house of Israel [Israel and Judah], and will be jealous for my holy name. ... When I have brought them again from the people, and gathered them out of their enemies' lands, and am sanctified in them in the sight of many nations; then shall they KNOW that I am the Lord their God ..." (Ezek. 39:25, 27-28)!

From this remarkable sequence of prophecy we can know that no war is foretold between the U.S.S.R. and America, or Canada, or Britain now!

ECONOMIC STRENGTH

GROSS NATIONAL PRODUCT
(thousand millions of US dollars)

United States	3765
Soviet Union	2067
Japan	1292
West Germany	697
France	540
United Kingdom	483
Italy	373
Canada	341
China	321
Poland	235

EXPORTS/IMPORTS
(thousand millions of US dollars)

	EXPORT	IMPORT
West Germany	243	191
United States	217	387
Japan	211	128
France	125	130
United Kingdom	107	126
Italy	98	99
Soviet Union	97	89
Canada	90	86
Netherlands	81	76
Belgium/Luxembourg	69	69

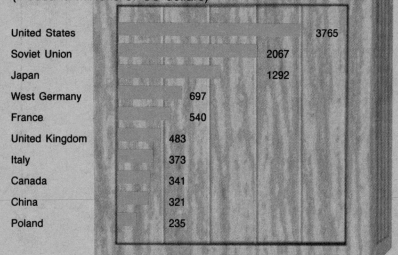

MILITARY SPENDING
(thousand millions of US dollars)

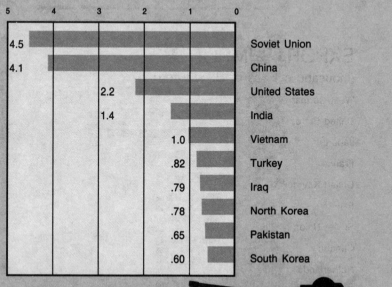

Country	Spending
Soviet Union	260
United States	237
United Kingdom	25.4
China	24.0
West Germany	22.8
France	22.4
Saudi Arabia	22.2
Iraq	14.6
Poland	13.4
Japan	12.7

0 50 100 150 200 300

5 4 3 2 1 0

Country	Armed Forces
Soviet Union	4.5
China	4.1
United States	2.2
India	1.4
Vietnam	1.0
Turkey	.82
Iraq	.79
North Korea	.78
Pakistan	.65
South Korea	.60

ARMED FORCES
(millions of persons)

MILITARY PREPAREDNESS

RUSSIAN AND SOVIET MANPOWER LOSSES IN THE 20TH CENTURY

The character of the peoples inhabiting what is now called the Soviet Union has been shaped by a historical fabric interwoven with a rich culture and endured tragedy. From the Mongol conquests of the 13th century, the Pugachev Rebellion of 1773 and Napoleon's invasion in 1812, to the First and Second World Wars and the Russian Revolution and Civil War, invasion and internal strife have molded a mindset of passionate patriotism and suspicion of foreigners.

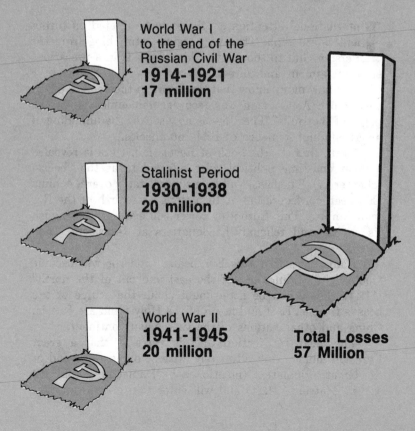

World War I
to the end of the
Russian Civil War
1914-1921
17 million

Stalinist Period
1930-1938
20 million

World War II
1941-1945
20 million

**Total Losses
57 Million**

SOUTH ASIA
IN PROPHECY

International attention continues to be riveted on turbulent South Asia. That vast region—stretching from the Persian Gulf to the South China Sea—is in a precarious state of ferment and unrest.

Yet how many know that the future of the peoples of the vast South Asia region was recorded millennia ago in the pages of the Bible? The stage is now set for the unfolding of an astounding sequence of Bible prophecies.

Turn, first, to the book of Revelation. Here is revealed a great end-time political ruler referred to as the "beast" (chapter 17). The beast will be a superdictator over a coming European confederation of 10 nations—a rebirth of the Roman Empire. This European power will eventually establish its capital and religious headquarters at Jerusalem (Dan. 11:45).

Daniel says that this European conqueror will become troubled by "tidings out of the east and out of the north" (11:44). There can be little doubt about the source of the beast's trouble. East and north of the Holy Land are Russia, China and other nations of the vast Asian continent.

The clear implication of this verse is that a great Eurasian alliance will ultimately arise at or near the end of the Great Tribulation (mentioned by Daniel in chapter 12 and in Matthew 24:21) and will enter into a confrontation with the restored Roman Empire. Much of Asia will eventually be marshaled into a great end-time, communist-dominated confederacy—encompassing nearly *one half* of the earth's population!

These atheist-led Asian armies are also described in Ezekiel, chapters 38 and 39, where elements of those forces are prophesied to invade the Holy Land when all 12 tribes of Israel have returned.

Misunderstood Prophecy

Some Bible scholars assert falsely that these prophecies of Ezekiel were fulfilled anciently. They never were. Others believe they are about to occur—but some years *before* Armageddon. Both views are erroneous.

The events of Ezekiel 38 and 39 are without question still future—for the "latter days" (38:16) and "latter years" (38:8). Moreover, Ezekiel 38:14 describes the time setting as being "in that day when my people of Israel dwelleth safely." This is certainly not the situation in the State of Israel today! The Israel described by Ezekiel is a nation that dwells in security, in *unwalled villages,* totally unprepared for war (38:8, 11, 14). Read it for yourself! These circumstances will be extant only *after* the coming of the Messiah, when surviving Eurasian forces will be supernaturally punished.

Asian alliances, however, will begin taking shape well in advance—and are *even now* beginning to move into their prophesied end-time configuration!

Table of Nations

The composition of the army that will come against the restored 12 tribes of Israel is clearly defined:

The account begins in Ezekiel 38:1-2: "And the word of the Lord came to me: Son of man, set your face against Gog, of the land of Magog, the prince of Rosh, of Meshech, and Tubal, and prophesy against him" (*The Amplified Bible*).

Here is a great power that will challenge the very rule of Christ!

Ezekiel reveals that joined with Magog, Rosh, Meshech and Tubal in this confederacy will be Persia, Cush, Phut (incorrectly rendered "Libya" in the *Authorized Version*),

Gomer and Togarmah (see verses 5-6). Who are these peoples today? And what do these prophecies have to do with the future of South Asia?

With the exception of Persia, the names mentioned by Ezekiel are nowhere to be found as names of nations on world maps today. The names of the majority of the world's modern nations are of fairly recent origin. Nations and peoples have undergone sometimes dozens of name changes over the centuries and millennia of history.

In the Bible, nations are named after their ancestors. Nations are families grown big. The whole human family of today, according to the Bible, springs from Shem, Ham and Japheth, the sons of Noah (Gen. 10:32). The "Table of Nations" of Genesis 10 is an account of the origins of today's nations and races.

Through migrations, these diverse peoples overspread the entire earth. You can read the story in Genesis 11. In many cases we can accurately trace their travels from the starting point of Babel (in what today is Iraq) through the pages of history to their present locations.

Especially helpful in such research are the accounts of the classical historians and geographers (such as Herodotus); Persian, Tatar and Arabic histories (such as *Meadows of Gold* by al-Masudi); the works of early Jewish historians (such as Josephus); Chinese and other Asian traditions; and medieval European chronicles.

Modern scholars generally give little credence to the Table of Nations or to many of these early histories and traditions. Consequently they are ignorant of the true identities of many of the world's peoples today.

Let us look again at the names mentioned by Ezekiel. Where are these peoples found today?

Gog of the Land of Magog

Ruling over all these allied peoples is Gog. Gog (meaning "mountain" *or* "high") is described as a great prince, the political/military head of the vast region in question. Ezekiel pictures Gog as a guard and commander over the assembled peoples (38:7).

Along with the beast, the miracle-working false prophet

RUSSIA AND SOUTH ASIA
3 of every 5 people live here

U.S.S.R.

MONGOLIA

N. KOREA

JAPAN

IRAN

AFGHANISTAN

S. KOREA

CHINA

PAKISTAN

NEPAL

BHUTAN

TAIWAN

INDIA

HONG KONG

BURMA

LAOS

BANGLADESH

THAILAND

VIETNAM

SRI LANKA

KAMPUCHEA

PHILIPPINES

BRUNEI

MALAYSIA

SINGAPORE

INDONESIA

POPULATION

MORE THAN 500,000,000
60,000,000 — 500,000,000
20,000,000 — 60,000,000
10,000,000 — 20,000,000
UP TO 10,000,000
POPULATION DENSITY OF MORE THAN 260 PER
SQUARE MILE, OR MORE THAN 100 PER SQUARE KM.

(Rev. 16:13; 19:20), and the leaders of an Arab-Muslim confederacy, Gog is one of the major end-time personalities
specifically mentioned in the Bible.

Gog is also a people, apparently a tribal subdivision of
Magog. The original Gog was probably a son or grandson of
Magog. Ezekiel describes the end-time Gog as being *of* the
land of Magog. How,
then, do we identify
Magog today? The
Table of Nations lists
Magog as the second
son of Japheth, son of
Noah.

> ## The prophecy of Ezekiel clearly indicates that Iran will eventually become linked with the Soviet Union.

Japheth's descen-
dants are primarily
Eurasian peoples.
They include the East
Slavs—Great Rus-
sians, Little Russians,
White Russians—and
the Mongoloid peoples of Asia outside of the Near East and
the subcontinent of India.

Japheth's son Magog gradually become divided into two
main branches. The western, Caucasian-looking Slavic
branch is identified by the first-century Jewish historian
Josephus and others as among the nomadic Scythian tribes
north of the Black Sea in what today is the Soviet Union.

But there was also an eastern or Mongoloid branch of
the Scythians that anciently inhabited the plains stretching
all the way to north China. The Venetian traveler Marco
Polo, who visited the Mongol realms in the 13th century,
identified Magog as being part of the Munguls or Mongols.
Other histories identify Magog with the Mandarin-speaking
northern Chinese. (The Cantonese-speaking southern Chinese, incidentally, are an Asian branch of Javan, another of
Japheth's sons.)

Which branch of Magog is intended in the prophecy of
Ezekiel? The Magog of Ezekiel 38 and 39 is pictured as a
people of a *northern* locality—i.e., the vast lands of the
Soviet Union. Ezekiel describes Gog as coming "from the

north parts" (39:2). The Soviet Union is in the far north.

Moreover, Gog is described as the prince of Rosh, Meshech and Tubal, peoples clearly *Russian* by descent.

Russians—Great and White

The Hebrew word *Rosh* is translated "chief" in Ezekiel 38:2-3 in the *Authorized Version*. In Hebrew, the word for chief is *Rosh*. But in Ezekiel's prophecy the original Hebrew may also be a proper name.

Rosh is the ancient Hebrew name for the Russ ("blonds") who settled in the plains of Eastern Europe in the ninth century, A.D. They gave their name to the Russian nation. The people of Rosh are among the *White Russians* of Byelorussia today.

Living next to the people of Rosh are Meshech and Tubal. Both Meshech and Tubal are sons of Japheth (Gen. 10:2) and thus brothers of Magog. To Herodotus and other classical geographers and historians they were known as the *Moskhi* or *Moschi* and the *Tibareni,* occupying the region of the Caucasus between the Black and Caspian Seas. In Assyrian inscriptions they are the *Muska* and *Tubla.* Josephus calls them the *Moschevi* and *Thobelites.*

The descendants of Meshech (Moskhi) ultimately traveled into the lands north of the Black Sea, settling around *Moscow.* They gave their name to that city, as well as to the *Moskva* River and the state of *Muscovy.*

Part of Tubal also moved north, giving their name to the river *Tobol* and founding the Siberian city of *Tobol*sk. (Mongoloid branches of Tubal are found in Tibet, Nepal, Bhutan, Sikkim, the Indian state of Nagaland, Xinkiang or Chinese Turkestan, and parts of northern China and Manchuria, according to Arabic sources.)

Together, the Caucasian branches of Meshech and Tubal form the two distinctive branches of the Great Russians of today. The Great Russians are the largest ethnic group of the Soviet Union.

Future Russo/China Alliance?

Ultimately allied with the Russians under Gog will be "many people" (Ezek. 38:6, 9, 15).

*Scenes in turbulent
South Asia: Guerrillas
of communist New
People's army train in
remote area of the
Philippines (top); Muslim
guerrillas opposing
Soviets in Afghanistan
pose with captured
Soviet armored vehicle
(below); Iraqi troops
guard Iranian prisoners
taken in the Iran-Iraq
war (facing page).*

These could hardly exclude the militarily weaker Chinese and their Asiatic kinsmen—those eastern Magogites who "dwell securely in the coastlands" of the Pacific (39:6, *The Amplified Bible*).

The People's Republic of China—the "many people" of Ezekiel 38—is thus pictured as being linked with Gog in the last days. We can conclude that, one way or another, the breach that separates the Soviet Union and China will eventually be bridged. Beijing and Moscow will yet come to terms in spite of racial and political tensions!

Linked with the Russians and the other nations of the Orient in the vast end-time Asian confederacy will be Persia, Cush, Phut, Gomer and Togarmah (Ezek. 38:5-6). Who are these peoples today?

History and Scripture identify them as the very peoples of the South Asian region. Willingly or unwillingly, they will all be drawn into the Soviet sphere of influence in the years just ahead! Let us look at each one individually.

Let us begin with Persia (Ezek. 38:5), the most easily identified. Persia is simply another name for modern-day Iran. The name *Persia* originated from a geographical region within southern Iran. This region was anciently known as Persis, the Greek form of Old Persian *Parsa*. Historically, the people of Iran have never used the name *Persia* for their country. They have always called it Iran, "Land of the Aryans." (*Aryan* is used to designate speakers of Indo-Iranian languages, as distinct from Semitic-speaking Arabs, for example.) The name *Iran*, however, did not come into widespread use in the west until the 1930s.

Iran today has a population of some 45 million. Iranians comprise nearly 70 percent of the country. Iranians, though Islamic, are totally distinct from the neighboring Arab peoples of the Middle East. They are a mixed people of the

Pavlovsky—Sygma

remnants of Media and Elam and other ancestors of Semitic and Hamitic stock.

Modern Iran also includes numerous minority groups of varying ethnic backgrounds: Turks, Kurds, Arabs, Baluchis, Armenians, Lurs, Azerbaijanis, Bakhtiaris and others.

There is growing evidence of a Soviet attempt to utilize to their own advantage disputes among certain of these ethnic minorities within Iran. Some observers see this activity as aimed at precipitating an internal crisis—a crisis that could provide an opportunity for Soviet military "intervention" in Iran.

An appeal for help by any pro-Soviet ethnic minorities in Iran could be answered by a movement of Soviet troops both from the Soviet Union across Iran's northern border and from Afghanistan across Iran's eastern border. Alternately, a pro-Soviet government might ultimately rise to power in Tehran and move the country into the Soviet orbit by nonviolent means.

Whatever the method, the prophecy of Ezekiel clearly indicates that Iran will eventually become linked with the Soviet Union. This is not to say that Iran or other South Asian nations will be incorporated into the Soviet Union as full-fledged republics. Rather, there will generally be only political linkage in the form of alliances or as vassal states dominated by Moscow.

Afghanistan, of course, is already in the Soviet orbit. A Soviet-installed regime today governs in Kabul.

Known anciently as Ariana and Bactria, and in the Middle Ages as Khorasan, Afghanistan lies in the very heart of Asia. Historically, the great invasions of the Indian subcontinent have been made through its strategic mountain passes.

Afghanistan's present racially mixed population is a reflection of its location astride the ancient trade and invasion routes of Central Asia. The bulk of the population (60 percent) is Pushtun or Pathan, the main tribes being the Durrani and the Ghilzai. Other groups represented are the Tajiks or Tadhziks (30 percent), Uzbeks (5 percent), Hazaras, Turkomans and Kirghiz.

The unifying factor amid all this ethnic diversity is

religion. Afganistan is almost wholly Islamic, mostly Sunni. Moslem armies had gained control of Afganistan as early as A.D. 652.

The biblical origins of the Afghan peoples are widely varied. Some are traced to the sons of Japheth. (The Turkomans, for example, claim descent from Tiras, a son of Japheth.) Others descend from branches of the families of Joktan, of Gomer, of Uz and of Esau. Some Afghan chronicles even claim that elements of the Pathans are descended by intermarriage from King Saul of ancient Israel through his grandson Afghana.

Also predicted to cluster around the banner of Gog in the latter days are *Cush* and *Phut* (or *Put*). These peoples of Ezekiel 38:5 are generally found today in the region of India and Pakistan.

Cush was a son of Ham (Gen. 10:6). Cush is often translated "Ethiopia" in the Bible. But not all Cushites live in Ethiopia!

The descendants of Cush split into two major groups, the Eastern and Western Cushites. The Western Cushites are found in major areas of Black Africa today, including modern Ethiopia, now under Soviet influence.

The Eastern Cushites, on the other hand, are the brown peoples of central and southern India and part of Ceylon (Sri Lanka). They are represented by such groups as the Dravidians, Tamils and Telugus. Herodotus calls these Eastern Cushites "Asiatic Ethiopians." During their migrations, incidentally, these Asiatic Cushites gave their name to the Hindu *Kush* mountain range of Central Asia.

Interestingly, the names of Cush's sons Seba and Raamah (Gen. 10:7) have been perpetuated in the Hindu god *Siva* or *Shiva* (the destroyer) and the hero *Rama* (an avatar of the god Vishnu).

Phut was also a son of Ham. Phut is often translated "Libya" in the Bible, referring to the land of Libya in North Africa. As with Cush, there is also an Asiatic branch of the family of Phut or Put. It is that Asiatic branch that will eventually become associated with the U.S.S.R.

Along with elements of Shem, descendants of Phut (or Put) were among the Indo-Aryans who settled northern India and drove the Cushitic Dravidians into the south of India in the second millennium B.C. The warrior-caste Raj*puts* were rulers over the historic region of Rajputana, a former group of princely states comprising what is now Rajasthan state of northwestern India.

Elements of Phut are also found today in other states of northern and central India and in the neighboring countries of Pakistan and Bangladesh. The clear implication, therefore, is that these nations will ultimately become politically associated with the U.S.S.R.

India, along with China, will undoubtedly contribute heavily to the 200 million-man army of Revelation 9:16. After one-thousand-million-strong communist China, India has the largest population of any country in the world (more than 750 million!).

The nation of India is officially a neutralist state aspiring to a nonaligned stand between the superpowers. But in light of India's long and often tension-ridden borders with China and Pakistan, the Soviet Union has become necessary insurance for New Delhi. India leans on Soviet protection to counterbalance the alliance of China and Pakistan.

India is heavily dependent on the Kremlin for key military supplies. New Delhi has a friendship treaty with Moscow, signed in 1971. And the Soviet Union has become India's major trading partner.

The government of Pakistan—lying to the east and south of Soviet-occupied Afghanistan—is growing more nervous by the day.

Pakistan now stands as the only obstacle between the Soviet troops in Afghanistan and Moscow's goal of a warm-water Arabian Sea port. By virtue of the Soviet military presence in Afghanistan, the Kremlin is now in a prime position to exert political and military pressure on Pakistan.

The Muslim nation of Pakistan consists of four provinces, two on each side of the Indus River. The two provinces on the eastern side—*Punjab* and *Sind*—are firmly in the control of President Zia ul-Haq's government in Islamabad.

The two provinces west of the Indus—*North-West Frontier* and *Baluchistan*—are in a state of unrest. These provinces share a 1,200-mile border with Soviet-occupied Afghanistan. The Pakistani government fears that the Soviets may now use Afghanistan as a base to exploit the separationist sentiments among the ethnic groups in these two provinces. Trouble among these ethnic minorities is already straining Pakistan's unity.

Of primary concern is the long-simmering independence movement among the Baluchi tribesmen of western Pakistan. The Baluchis have long sought to unite with fellow tribesmen in southern Afghanistan and eastern Iran to form an independent state of Baluchistan.

There is strong evidence of deep Soviet involvement in this effort to carve out a separate Baluchi state. A pro-Russian vassal state in Baluchistan would effectively extend Soviet influence all the way south to the Arabian Sea. The Kremlin would at last have the warm-water ports that it has sought since the days of the czars.

As an added bonus, the Soviets would be in a position to control the major oil supply lines leading from the Persian Gulf!

Pushtu-speaking tribesmen in northwestern Pakistan and eastern Afghanistan have also long dreamed of their own independent state of Pushtunistan. These peoples, like the Baluchis, provide potentially fertile soil for Soviet revolutionary propaganda.

> **In the Bible, nations are named after their ancestors. Nations are families grown big.**

The predominantly Muslim nation of Bangladesh—once known as East Pakistan—broke away from Pakistan in a bloody civil war in 1971. Though Bangladesh officially adheres to the principle of nonalignment, its relations with the Soviet Union have grown steadily closer.

Also allied with Gog will be "Gomer, Togarmah and all their bands" (Ezek. 38:6).

Gomer was the eldest son of Japheth. Contrary to the

assertions of many students of Bible prophecy, Gomer in this prophecy is not West Germany.

Who, then, is Gomer? Among the Oriental descendants of Gomer's three sons are found elements of the Turkic and Tatar (Turko-Mongol) peoples of the Asian steppes and deserts.

Many of these peoples—inhabiting the five socialist republics of Soviet Central Asia—have already been incorporated into the U.S.S.R. The nation of Mongolia, wedged between the Soviet Union and China in the region just south of Siberia, is a virtual Soviet satellite. The Turkic Uighurs of Xinkiang (western China) and the Mongols of Inner Mongolia are under Communist Chinese control.

Gomer's third son, Togarmah, is specifically mentioned in Ezekiel 38. Togarmah, in part, settled ancient Armenia. Descendants of Togarmah also migrated eastward into Mongolia, where they are today found mixed with elements of Magog. Togarmah's modern-day descendants are also found in China's Xinkiang province and in Russian Siberia or Tartary.

Ezekiel, however, speaks specifically of Togarmah "in the uttermost parts of the north" (38:6, *Amplified*). This is a clear reference to the *Siberian* branch of Togarmah.

But what of Southeast Asia?

The modern-day nations of this region are of the southern Mongoloid racial group. These nations are primarily Japhetic in descent, of the line of Gomer and, farther east, of Javan. Here communism has already deeply penetrated.

Vietnam is already a communist nation in the Soviet fold. After some two decades of fighting, the American-backed government of South Vietnam surrendered to Soviet-supported North Vietnamese forces in the spring of 1975. Within days the communist conquest of South Vietnam was effectively completed. Vietnam was officially reunited as a communist state in July 1976.

The government of neighboring Laos is an ally of Vietnam and the Soviet Union. Nearby Cambodia (Kampuchea) has been dominated by Vietnam since 1979.

Continuing Vietnamese military activity within Cambodia poses a potential threat to the security of Thailand to the north and west. Malaysia also sees a potential military menace from expansionist Vietnam. Adding to the uncertainty, small bands of communist guerrillas continue to roam the Thai-Malaysia border area.

In Burma, militarily active communist guerrillas are challenging the government in Rangoon. Insurgent uprisings among the country's ethnic minorities add to the instability in that nation. In Indonesia and the Philippines too, communist insurgency occasionally assails the authority of the central governments.

Most of Southeast Asia will undoubtedly find it difficult to withstand incessant communist pressure. Ultimately, prophecy reveals, the region will be forced into cooperating with the Soviet Union and her allies.

"I Am Against You!"

As we have seen, the coming Eurasian confederacy will devastate much of Western Europe. After Christ decimates the armies of all nations gathered at Armageddon, Gog will assemble a large army from among his surviving Eurasian forces. That army will attempt to impose its ideology on a restored Israel. But it will not succeed!

"Behold, I am against you, O Gog!" God declares (Ezek. 38:3). The fate of his armies is vividly portrayed: "You shall fall on the mountains of Israel, you and all your troops, and the peoples who are with you; I shall give you as food to every kind of predatory bird and beast of the field" (Ezek. 39:4, *Amplified*). The people of Israel will labor seven months burying the millions of Gog's dead (39:12). The survivors will know that God rules.

The demise of Gog and his allies will furnish a powerful witness to the nations of the world. "And I shall set My glory among the nations; and all the nations will see My judgment which I have executed," God declares (39:21, *Amplified*).

The people of Israel will utterly destroy the weapons carried by Gog's army (39:9-10). With the power of Gog irretrievably broken, the nations of the world will at last submit to the government of God. After 6,000 years of war and international strife, worldwide peace will finally become reality. "And they shall beat their swords into plowshares, and their spears into pruninghooks: nation shall not lift up sword against nation, neither shall they learn war any more" (Mic. 4:3; Isa. 2:4).

South Asia—and the world—will at last know true peace!

YOU *CAN* UNDERSTAND THE BIBLE!

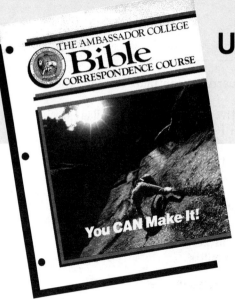

When you read the Bible, do you find it *difficult* to understand — even CONFUS-ING? You're not alone if you do. Most people do not understand the Bible today!

Why?

One major reason is because not *all* the truth on any one subject is found in any one place in the Bible. To properly UNDERSTAND the Word of God, you must put together ALL the scriptures on a particular subject. "Here a little, and there a little"! (Isa. 28:10, 13.) And only when all the scriptures are put together can you *really* see what the Bible says.

That's why we offer the Ambassador College Correspondence Course. This unique course of bib-lical understanding is a totally *different* method of Bible study. It makes the Bible *easy* to understand. It shows how the Bible is the FOUNDATION of knowledge. It explains why millions have *totally* mis-understood the Bible — why even many theologians are confused about what it teaches.

This course is absolutely *free!* There is no tu-ition. Just write to one of the addresses listed on the last page of this booklet and ask for the first lesson.

Where Are We NOW in Prophecy?

You've heard them all: Armageddon. The Second Coming. The beast. The number 666. The Great Tribulation. The Day of the Lord.

What do these seemingly strange biblical symbols mean? Is it possible to know? Can you understand Bible prophecy?

Yes! We have prepared for you, in understandable language, an overview of biblical prophecy—the neglected one-third of your Bible. All you have to do to receive your free copy of "Where Are We Now in Prophecy?" is to send your request to one of the addresses on the reverse of this page. Do it now while it is on your mind!

MAILING ADDRESSES WORLDWIDE

United States: Worldwide Church of God, Pasadena, California 91123

United Kingdom, rest of Europe and Middle East: The Plain Truth, P.O. Box 111, Borehamwood, Herts, England WD6 1LU

Canada: Worldwide Church of God, P.O. Box 44, Station A, Vancouver, B.C. V6C 2M2

Canada (French language): Le Monde à Venir, B.P. 121, Succ. A, Montreal, P. Q. H3C 1C5

Mexico: Institución Ambassador, Apartado Postal 5-595, 06502 Mexico D.F.

South America: Institución Ambassador, Apartado Aéreo 11430, Bogotá 1, D.E., Colombia

Caribbean: Worldwide Church of God, G.P.O. Box 6063, San Juan, Puerto Rico 00936-6063

France: Le Monde à Venir, B.P. 64, 75662 Paris Cédex 14

Switzerland: Le Monde à Venir, Case Postale 10, 91 rue de la Servette, CH-1211 Genève 7, Suisse

Italy: La Pura Verità, Casella Postale 10349 00144 Roma EUR, Italia

Germany: Ambassador College, Postfach 1129, D-5300 Bonn 1, West Germany

Holland and Belgium: Ambassador College, Postbus 444, 3430 AK Nieuwegein, Nederland

Belgium: Le Monde à Venir, B.P. 31, 6000 Charleroi 1, Belgique

Denmark: The Plain Truth, Box 211, DK-8100 Aarhus C

Norway: The Plain Truth, Postboks 2513 Solli, N-0203 Oslo 2

Sweden: The Plain Truth, Box 5380, S-102 46, Stockholm

Australia: Worldwide Church of God, P.O. Box 202, Burleigh Heads, Queensland 4220

India: Worldwide Church of God, P.O. Box 6727, Bombay 400 052, India

Sri Lanka: Worldwide Church of God, P.O. Box 1824, Colombo, Sri Lanka

Malaysia: Worldwide Church of God, P.O. Box 430, Jalan Sultan, 46750 Petaling Jaya, Selangor, Malaysia

Singapore: Worldwide Church of God, P.O. Box 111, Farrer Road Post Office, Singapore 9128

New Zealand and the Pacific Isles: Ambassador College, P.O. Box 2709, Auckland 1, New Zealand

The Philippines: Worldwide Church of God, P.O. Box 1111, Makati, Metro Manila, Philippines 3117

Israel: Ambassador College, P.O. Box 19111, Jerusalem

South Africa: Ambassador College, P.O. Box 5644, Cape Town 8000

Zimbabwe: Ambassador College, Box UA30, Union Avenue, Harare, Zimbabwe

Nigeria: Worldwide Church of God, PMB 21006, Ikeja, Lagos State, Nigeria

Ghana: Worldwide Church of God, P.O. Box 9617, Kotoka International Airport, Accra

Kenya: Worldwide Church of God, P.O. Box 47135, Nairobi

Mauritius and Seychelles: Ambassador College, P.O. Box 888, Port Louis, Mauritius